snoopy's
facts & fun book about boats

387 P

SNOOPY 21

Based on the Charles M. Schulz Characters

Random House   New York

Designed by Terry Flanagan

You can make a raft from just about anything that floats. The first rafts were made thousands of years ago, probably by tying logs together.

Long ago, many
American Indians
made light canoes
from thin pieces of
wood and the bark of
birch trees. Today
some of the best
canoes are still made
of birch bark.

In a rowboat the rower sits backward!
The harder the rower pulls the oars, the
faster the boat goes.

In the cold north some Eskimos fish from
kayaks. The top of a kayak is tightly covered
to keep out the ice-cold water.

The canals of Venice, Italy, are like streets of water. Visitors often travel around town in fancy taxi-boats called gondolas.

A sailboat runs on wind power. Wind blows against the sails and pushes the boat along. When a sailor moves the tiller, the rudder moves—and the boat turns.

A catamaran is like two boats that share one set of sails. Two thin hulls help make the catamaran very fast and help keep the boat from tipping over.

Dhows are Arab sailing
ships. They have graceful
triangle-shaped sails.

A junk is a Chinese ship sometimes used for fishing. People often live on their junks, too.

Most people who live in houseboats do not move them from place to place. Houseboats have kitchens, beds, and just about everything that land houses have!

Steamboats used to carry passengers up and down lakes and rivers. The steamboats had big turning paddle wheels at the back or sides.

On some rivers and lakes you can still ride on a paddle steamer—just for fun!

A trawler drags a huge net along the bottom of the ocean. The net catches fish that live near the ocean floor.

After the net is pulled up, the fish are cleaned and frozen right on the fishing boat.

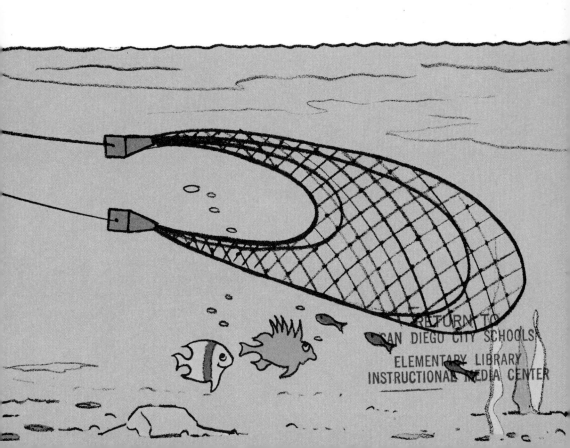

Zoom! An outboard motor can be attached to almost any small boat to make it go fast.

POOCHIE

NO DOGS
ALLOWED
ON THIS
BEACH!

Icebreakers have extra-strong engines and hulls to help them cut through thick ice. They clear a path for other ships.

Supertankers carry huge loads of oil from place to place. Some supertankers are longer than three football fields put together!

Crews aboard these big tankships must be very careful not to spill any oil that could make the ocean dirty.

Hovercraft speed along above the water on a cushion of air. They can travel over land, too!

Big flat barges carry heavy loads. Some
take garbage far out to sea for dumping.
Many barges have no engines of their
own. Tugboats with engines pull them along.
Tugboats are small, but they are so strong
that they can pull many barges at once!

Tugboats can also help a giant ocean liner get in and out of the harbor to load and unload its passengers. Tugs push and pull the big ship, steering it through the crowded harbor.

Taking a cruise on an ocean liner is fun!
An ocean liner has bedrooms, restaurants,
swimming pools, game rooms, and theaters.
It is like a huge floating hotel.

Sometimes there is a fire on a ship or on a dock where ships load and unload. Then a fireboat hurries to help. The fireboat's big water guns spray water onto the fire to put it out.

If a ship has an accident, a Coast Guard cutter rushes to the rescue!

A submarine is a ship that can travel under water. A long tube called a periscope lets people inside the submarine see what is happening above the surface of the water.

Wherever there is an ocean or a lake or a river, you will usually find boats or ships. And big or small, they are both useful and lots of fun.